THE LIFE OF CHRIST REVEALED

THE LIFE OF
CHRIST
REVEALED

The Visions of Blessed Veronica of Milan

Translated by Fr. Robert Nixon, OSB

TAN Books
Gastonia, North Carolina

Translated by Fr. Robert Nixon, OSB

Cover design by Jordan Avery

Cover image: Church of Turago Bordone: *Beata Veronica*. Fresco by Luigi Migliavacca. G. Scuri, CC BY-SA 3.0 <https://creativecommons.org/licenses/by-sa/3.0>, via Wikimedia Commons.

Interior Image: *Representation of St. Veronica of Milan*, Binasco (1445–1497). 19th century, engraving. Private Collection, Photo © The Holbarn Archive / Bridgeman Images.

ISBN: 978-1-5051-3342-4
Kindle ISBN: 978-1-5051-3434-6
ePUB ISBN: 978-1-5051-3435-3

Published in the United States by
TAN Books
PO Box 269
Gastonia, NC 28053
www.TANBooks.com

Printed in India

“Blessed are the pure in heart,
for they shall see God.”

—Matthew 5:8

CONTENTS

TRANSLATOR'S INTRODUCTION

Blessed Veronica of Milan was a nun, mystic, and visionary of the late Middle Ages. In her relatively short life, her virtue, sanctity, and divine love inspired and touched all those whom she encountered. She was born in 1445 to a poor but devoutly Catholic peasant family in the village of Binasco,[1] close to Milan.

From an early age, she felt a vocation to a life of prayer and service of the Lord, and so for a long time earnestly sought admission to the Augustinian Convent of Saint Martha in Milan to be a nun. But the Mother-Superior of the convent noted that Veronica was almost illiterate and urged her to learn reading and writing before applying again. So, the devout maiden prayed to Christ and to the Blessed Virgin, pleading that they should assist her in learning letters. As her prayer concluded, suddenly Mary appeared to her in a splendid vision. She told Veronica that she would teach her literacy, but there were only

1 Because of this, Veronica is sometimes referred to as "Blessed Veronica of Binasco."

three letters she needed to know. There appeared then to Veronica three letters—one white, one black, and one red. The Mother of God then told her what these letters meant. The white letter signified purity of heart, the black letter signified thinking ill of others and judging them for their faults, and the red letter signified daily meditation on the passion of Christ.

The Queen of Heaven said, "If you remember just these three letters, my daughter, you will know all you need to be pleasing to my Son! For whoever maintains purity of heart shines before Him radiantly. But whoever thinks ill of others and judges and condemns them for their failings becomes black and foul in the sight of God. And, finally, whoever meditates daily on the passion of Christ will be inflamed with the fire of divine love and will glow like a brilliant and beautiful flame in His sight."

Veronica then decided to enroll in the convent as a lay sister. Lay sisters were a class of nuns who were generally illiterate and of humble birth. They were not bound to the full liturgical observance of the Divine Office, since that required the ability to read Latin fairly fluently. They would typically be assigned the more lowly domestic duties within the convent, acting almost as servants to the fully professed sisters. Veronica accepted this vocation with genuine commitment and joy.

Devoting herself very intensely to prayer and contemplation, she soon began to experience a remarkable series of visions concerning the life of Christ. Although she did not reveal the full contents of all her visions, she shared many of them with one of her fellow nuns, a certain Sister Thadea. Sister Thadea, in turn, related them to Fr. Isidor Isolanus, of the Order of Preachers, who wrote a life of Blessed Veronica in 1518. It is this biography of Blessed Veronica (reproduced in the *Acta Sanctorum* for January 13), which is the source text for the translation offered in this book, *The Visions of Blessed Veronica of Milan*.

Blessed Veronica, though deeply humble, steadily acquired a reputation for charity, sanctity, and wisdom during her lifetime; and the power of the Lord manifested itself in many miracles worked through her prayers and intercessions. After her death in 1497, she immediately began to be venerated as a saint by her own convent and by the local population. This local veneration was formally confirmed and approved by Pope Leo X in 1517. In 1672, the veneration of Veronica of Milan as one of the beatified was extended to the entire Catholic Church by Pope Clement X.

Blessed Veronica's visions faithfully reflect the accounts of the life of Our Lord found in the Gospels. Yet, in many cases, they add beautiful and touching details of color, imagery, and emotion. These details fill out many of the basic Gospel narratives, and they often harmonize the accounts of the different Evangelists. In many ways, they may be compared with the visions of Blessed Anne Catherine Emmerich, although they precede them by some 350 years.

Within these pages, readers will encounter a multitude of striking and fascinating descriptions, including details of the arduous journey of the Holy Family to Egypt, and their encounters with gangs of bandits along the way; a description of the food, costumes, and even dancing at the wedding feast at Cana; and many of the private thoughts and feelings of both Jesus and the Blessed Virgin Mary. The passion of Christ, in particular, is described in a most heartrending and poignant manner.

It is the sincere hope of the translator that these visions, offered here in English translation for the first time, will renew for many readers the wonder of the Gospel narrative ("the greatest story ever told") in a beautiful and memorable manner, and that it may stir up the same fire of divine love, contemplation, and devotion that burned so ardently in the heart of Blessed Veronica.

Beata Veronica, ora pro nobis!

Fr. Robert Nixon, OSB
Abbey of the Most Holy Trinity,
New Norcia, Western Australia

1

THE ANNUNCIATION OF THE LORD

On the solemnity of the Annunciation of the Lord,[2] Blessed Veronica was contemplating quietly in her cell when her spirit was led forth by an angel into the heavens. There she beheld all the indescribable beauty and power of the celestial court. Then the angel who had led her there spoke to Veronica, saying: "Look! There is the archangel Gabriel, the herald of God, who, for the sake of the salvation of the human race, announced on this day the Incarnation of Christ to the most Blessed Virgin.

"It was that glorious angel, Gabriel, who entered into her chamber, aglow with brilliant splendor. There he found the Virgin reading the Scriptures, and he greeted her, saying: 'Hail, full of grace! The Lord is with you. Blessed are you among women.' When Mary heard this, she was astonished and pondered on the meaning of this salutation. But the angel said to

[2] March 25.

her: 'Fear not, Mary, for you have found grace with God. Behold, you will conceive in your womb and bear a Son, and you shall call Him Jesus. And He will be great and called the Son of the Most High. And the Lord shall give unto Him the throne of his ancestor David, and His Kingdom will have no end! You are also to be acclaimed as the greatest of all women, for you shall be granted the titles and honors of the Queen of Heaven and the Mother of God!'

"Then Mary spoke to the angel, saying: 'But how can this come to be, since I have not known a man?' And the angel responded, saying those words which are recorded in the Gospel.[3] Then Mary exclaimed: 'Behold, the handmaid of the Lord! Be it done unto me according to your word.' And then she conceived the true Son of God, of the Holy Spirit. After a few days, Mary arose and went forth into the mountains.

"And know this," continued the angel to Veronica, "that Gabriel revealed to the Blessed Virgin all the future mysteries of her Son before He was born, including His passion, His joys, and His whole manner of life."

After this vision, Blessed Veronica returned to her normal senses. Later, while attending the sacred solemnity of the Mass, she reverently received the most Holy Body of Christ.

---

[3] See Lk 1:35:"The Holy Spirit will come upon you, and the power of the Most High will overshadow you; therefore the Child to be born will be holy; He will be called the Son of God."

2

THE NATIVITY OF THE LORD

Two days before the Solemnity of the Nativity of the Lord,[4] Blessed Veronica was resting on her bed at night when she found her soul taken up to the starry realms of heaven. There she saw the splendor of the celestial Jerusalem, adorned with unimaginable radiance and indescribable beauty. This heavenly city was of such immense magnitude that it seemed to be a thousand times larger than the entire earth, and it was filled with countless blessed souls and angels. Such was the beauty and majesty of the place that Veronica was unable to find any earthly words which could serve to describe it.

She could sense that the angels were all eager to express to her their superlative joy, just as human beings long to share their happiness with others. And she saw the portals of this celestial city, resplendent with gold of transcendent and blazing luster. But just at this point, Veronica was returned to her normal senses.

---

[4] December 23.

Then, on the night of Christmas Eve, Veronica was again taken up into a spiritual ecstasy. She beheld, this time, the Blessed Virgin Mary, evidently soon to deliver her Child, and seated upon a donkey. The Blessed Virgin appeared to be of tender years and of small stature, and therefore little more than a girl. Saint Joseph was present also, as was a maidservant, and a manservant who was leading an ox, bearing provisions for their journey.

Next, Veronica saw Mary (who was heavily pregnant) and Saint Joseph standing together, having their names recorded for the census. She noted that they signed themselves as a man and wife to the official. Their servants were absent at that point. The vision then ended, and Veronica returned to her usual consciousness.

In the morning, the Mother Abbess of the convent then summoned Veronica and sent her forth with another sister to beg for alms in the city of Milan, to help support the sisters.[5] On the evening of that same day (which was Christmas), Veronica again devoted herself to intense prayer. Without delay, her vision was resumed.

She saw once more the Blessed Virgin and Saint Joseph in Bethlehem, where she had seen them previously. They were wandering the streets, earnestly seeking for a place where they could be accommodated for the night. But, despite making many inquiries, they found nothing available to them at all.

---

[5] This seems to reflect the extreme poverty of Blessed Veronica's convent.

For such was the multitude gathered in Bethlehem for the census at that time that not a single room was to be had, and even the humble dwellings of poor widows were completely occupied with guests to their full capacity.

Saint Joseph was visibly anxious and saddened by this situation, for he realized that Mary was due to give birth very soon. Now at the time, the twilight of evening was fading to darkness, and night was falling fast. Joseph saw a small and primitive stable by the side of the road. And he said to Mary: "My dearest wife, it behooves us to find a place of shelter, for very soon it will be night. Let us enter that little stable over there, for it is the only place where we will have a roof over our heads." The Blessed Virgin promptly agreed to this and gracefully descended from her donkey.

She then said to Joseph: "Joseph, my time of delivery is drawing nigh!" At once, Joseph replied: "I will go and engage midwives and maidservants to assist you in the birth." But at this, Mary merely laughed gently at his noble intentions, and the unlikelihood of his fulfilling them. "Do not laugh, Mary, for this is a most serious matter!" said Joseph. "You are a first-time mother, and you may well need help in the delivery." And so, the noble Saint Joseph went forth into the silent darkness of the night.

At this point, Veronica's vision stopped, and she once more returned to her usual awareness of the external world. She realized then that it was now almost time for the Office of Vigils.[6] So, having completed these prayers, she returned to prayer and meditation until dawn.

She was soon drawn back to her vision. She saw the Blessed Mary still in the stable in which Joseph had placed her. But she saw with her also now the infant Jesus, the Savior of the world! He lay peacefully in the manger, and with one hand, He clasped lovingly His Mother, while with the other He held onto the straw in the manger. Then, holy Mary removed her own veil from her head and tore it cleanly in two. She used half of it to cover the small body of her newborn Son, and she placed the other half under Him to shield His sacred form from the straw upon which He rested.

Now Joseph, her husband, was not present at this time and had not been present at the time of the birth of Our Lord. But now, he arrived back, accompanied by three women. These three women were afraid to enter the stable, for it was filled with a brilliant and heavenly light, which glowed all around the infant Jesus and His glorious Mother in glorious splendor. But Saint Joseph himself went in with no hesitation and fell to his knees in adoration before the Son of Mary, whom he knew also to be the true Son of God.

Seeing Joseph enter, two of the women took courage and went inside also. But, the third was still hesitant and said: "I have heard the oracles that a most pure and immaculate Virgin

---

6 Probably sometime between 2:00–3:00 a.m.

would give birth to the Messiah. But unless I see it, I shall not believe!" And then she entered the stable and reached out her hand to touch the radiant Virgin Mother, as if to verify the reality of the virgin birth. And upon touching her, a burning sensation at once overcame the woman. And this fiery pain that seized upon her almost struck her down.[7]

Then, suddenly, an angel of the Lord appeared and spoke to the afflicted woman. "Ask for mercy from holy Mary," the angel said, "for doubting the truth which the prophets foretold about her! But now reach out your hand in adoration to touch the Son who has been born to her, and then you shall find relief." This she accordingly did, and as soon as she touched the baby Jesus, her pain instantly vanished. And the three women all went forth and proclaimed to everyone that the Savior of the world had indeed been born.

But, O Reader, let us return our attention to Jesus, lying in the manger. Blessed Veronica witnessed the celestial Virgin kneeling before Him, with her hands joining in adoring prayer. An ox and donkey were there in the stable, and these likewise venerated the Child on bended knees. An angel of the Lord was present too, who also worshipped Him most humbly. Indeed, above the stable there was an entire multitude of holy angels, who sang together in a glorious chorus: "Glory to God in the highest!"

---

7 This seems to correspond with an incident contained in *The Protoevangelium of James*, 19–20.

This song of the angelic multitude resonated through the entire celestial firmament, and it was of a beauty and complexity which transcended the capacity of mortal ears to hear or understand. And the stable in which Our Lord rested was bathed in a refulgent light, which illuminated the darkness of the night such that it shone more brightly than the height of day.

Now there were some shepherds in this region, keeping watch over their flocks during the long hours of the night. They perceived this inexplicable and miraculous light from a distance, and they were terrified and fell on their faces. But then an angel appeared to them, and the same heavenly radiance which they had seen also shone where they were situated. Their hearts were filled with astonishment and confusion, but that angel said: "Fear not, O shepherds! For, behold, I bring to you good news of the greatest joy. For in the city of David there has been born the One who is destined to be the Savior of the world! Go now, that you may worship Him! And this shall be the sign that you will see: an Infant wrapped in swaddling clothes and resting in a stable."

So, the shepherds hastened forth, bewildered and stupefied by all the marvels they had witnessed. And the flocks of sheep which they protected also followed them, as if eager to accompany them to worship the Infant Christ. Indeed, the angel of the Lord, who was there present, explained to Veronica that all created things—the stars, the sun, the moon, and even the beasts, birds, plants, and stones—were filled with an overwhelming desire to pay homage to their Incarnate Creator and eternal King.

The saintly virgin, Veronica, was amazing and awestruck by all of these things. She herself joined the others in adoring the holy Baby upon bended knees, but she felt utterly incapable of reaching out her hand to touch Him, or of uttering a single articulate word—such was the intensity of the love and awestruck wonder which she felt for Him. Veronica related that she also witnessed many other mysterious and marvelous things, but she did not desire to share these with anyone else, for they surpassed what was permitted to living humans to know, except by divine revelation.

In the days which followed Christmas, after Veronica had attended the Holy Sacrifice of the Mass three times and received each time the sacred Body of Christ, she was again taken up in a mystical ecstasy. She related that she was not permitted to disclose to anyone what she experienced and witnessed in these visions.

But she did say how, after receiving the Holy Eucharist, she had a vision of how the heavens themselves exulted in fervent jubilation at the birth of the Savior. It was as if they flowed with celestial honey and glowed with the radiant whiteness of freshly fallen snow. And a vast circle of resplendent gold appeared in the highest sphere of the firmament. Within this circle was the Virgin Queen, holding in her arms the Divine Infant. And though but a tender Baby, He spoke in words which were perfectly articulated and fully comprehensible to Veronica's ears. But as to what He said to her, she was silent; for, she explained, it was not permissible to repeat these secret words to any mortal ears.

3

THE CIRCUMCISION OF THE SAVIOR

While she was at Mass on the feast of the Circumcision of the Lord,[8] the soul of Blessed Veronica was raised up out of her physical senses, and she entered into a mystical trance. During that trance, she experienced a vision in which she was taken into a beautiful temple, adorned in most wondrous fashion. Veronica had no idea of where she was, but she became aware of the presence of an angel of the Lord standing beside her, who was there as a guide and companion to her.

There was in that temple an altar which was magnificently decorated. Before this altar stood an old man of very grave and venerable appearance. There was also present a certain very old widow, as well as many other onlookers of both sexes.

And then a certain man entered, bearing the Infant Jesus! The old man accepted the baby in his arms. The same man then came with two pairs of pigeons and two pairs of turtledoves,

8 January 1.

and he presented them to the old man. Meanwhile, Mother Mary and Joseph stood looking on from a distance, bearing a serious and anxious aspect.

Then the old man removed the swaddling clothes from the infant Jesus. Taking a sharp knife of stone, he performed the operation of circumcision upon the child. The Divine Infant was crying out in pain and wailing vehemently. This sight deeply touched the heart of the Virgin Mary, who cried out in a mournful voice, as if in agony herself from the wound inflicted by the knife.

At this point, Veronica returned to her normal awareness, but was affected with tears of heartfelt sorrow. She continued to be affected by deep sadness for the whole day, as if the voice of the little infant Jesus crying out in pain continued to resonate in her ears. Her tender heart was touched with the deepest compassion for the suffering both of the Christ-child as He underwent the painful operation of circumcision, and His glorious Mother as she looked on with infinite love and sympathy for her Son.

4

THE ADORATION OF THE MAGI

When Blessed Veronica was present at the Mass of the Epiphany of the Lord,[9] she was taken up into a trance and transported in spirit to one of the Eastern regions of the world. There she witnessed an angel of the Lord, who was speaking to the king of the region. The angel announced that a great King who was to be the Savior of the world had been born, and the angel urged him to go forth to pay homage to this newborn Savior and King.

And then, without delay, Veronica was taken in spirit to a different region of the world, also in the East. And she saw the same angel of the Lord communicate the same message and exhortation to the king of that region.

And then she was transported to yet another region in the East, this time even more remote than those previously. Again, the angel of the Lord was with her, and she witnessed

[9] January 6.

him proclaiming the same message to the monarch of this distant land.

At this point, the spirit and mind of Veronica were returned to her body, and she came out of her trance and returned to her normal senses.

But on the evening of that day, after the sun had set, when Veronica devoted herself to pray, she was again taken into a trance. The same angel took her to the realms of the East once more. She saw the three kings whom she had previously been shown separately now gathered together. They spoke among themselves and told each other how each of them had seen an angel, and they related the message which it had imparted to them. Each of the three kings spoke of how the angel had told them that a great King, who would become the Savior of the world, had been born.

The three kings of the East then resolved to travel together to seek this wondrous infant. "Let us go forth and pay our homage to Him!" they exclaimed. Next, Veronica witnessed them making preparations for their journey, gathering ample supplies and assembling a splendid royal retinue. Veronica was amazed to see the three dromedaries which they prepared to carry them—huge and powerful beasts, the like of which she had never beheld before. Finally, once everything had been made ready for their expedition, one of the kings asked: "But who shall lead us to the place where this newborn Monarch is to be found? Who or what shall show to us the way we must go?"

At this point, a brilliant star of greater luminosity than any other arose suddenly in the sky. The kings of the East witnessed this phenomenon with exceedingly great joy, for they were all learned in the lore of the stars, and they knew that nothing like this had ever appeared before. "Behold," they exclaimed, "this is the sign of the great King! Let us follow it, for it will surely lead us to Him."

And thus, they did, traveling far and long, through desert and forest, and over mountains and plains. Veronica attested that, with the angel of the Lord accompanying her, she saw these kings journey through many lands and regions, mounted upon their enormous dromedaries and followed by a large retinue of servants and beasts. And as she did, she was able to overhear the conversations of the three kings, as they speculated about where and who this newborn King might be and how He would become the Savior of the world.

At this point, Veronica's vision ended, and she was returned to her normal senses. Once dawn was past and the light of day shone brightly, Veronica attended the Mass which was being celebrated in the Church of Saint Martha.[10] After the elevation and adoration of the consecrated Sacrament, Veronica was once again drawn into a trance. She saw there the three kings of the East now in Jerusalem and in the presence the wicked King Herod. They were relating to him the message they had

---

[10] The previous Mass mentioned was perhaps the Vigil Mass of the Epiphany.

each received from an angel, and they were explaining to him that the star which had appeared had led them to the city of Jerusalem. It was obvious to Veronica that Herod was fuming with rage and consumed with bitter envy and fear. Yet, he cunningly concealed this from the visiting kings and pretended instead that he was overjoyed at the news of the birth of this future great King and Savior.

He ordered a sumptuous regal banquet to be prepared for his royal guests, and Herod and the three kings feasted together splendidly. And Veronica could hear them converse of many wondrous things, and in particular the significance and destiny of this newborn King.

At this point, Veronica emerged from her vision, to her usual senses. She perceived that the priest was now about to distribute Communion to those who were to receive the Blessed Sacrament on that day. And Blessed Veronica, together with a number of the other sisters, each received the most Holy Body of Christ. As she prayed after this, she was immediately drawn into another trance and her earlier vision continued.

This time, she perceived King Herod about to bid farewell to the Eastern kings. He spoke to them thus: "Go forth and inquire carefully about the infant, and then come back to me and tell me all you have discovered!" Veronica saw clearly how Herod pretended to be joyful and eager to support them, and how the kings of the East, in return, displayed their enthusiasm and wonder. But the holy maiden noticed also that the star which they had followed had disappeared at this time. So, the kings of the East said to each other, as they departed from Herod: "Now that this radiant star, our guiding light, has vanished, where should we go to next?"

But at that moment, the star which had appeared while they were in the East now reappeared with all its former brilliance. At this, they rejoiced exceedingly. And they followed it faithfully, until they arrived at the place where the holy infant was to be found. But before they approached that place, they dismounted from their dromedaries. Leaving their retinue of servants behind them, the three kings went forth on foot, bearing in their hands the bags containing their various gifts.

At this point, Blessed Veronica perceived an angel of the Lord appearing to Mary and announcing to her that these visitors from afar were about to arrive, to pay homage to the infant Jesus. Upon hearing this, Mary was greatly surprised and perplexed. Yet just then, the kings entered the stable. As they entered, Mary stood up. Then, falling to their knees, the kings firstly venerated the Blessed Virgin with deep humility and reverence. The holy Mother of God then sat down once more, placing her Son gently upon her lap. Jesus was wrapped in cloth, but the lower legs of the infant were uncovered and visible. Saint Joseph was also present, standing quietly in the background.

When they saw the Son of God, the three kings genuflected solemnly three times, touching their heads to the ground before

Him. Then they appeared to dispute among themselves about which of them should approach the newborn Savior first. And then the youngest of the three went forward. He removed the golden crown which he wore upon his head and placed it on the ground before the holy infant. With the greatest reverence and love, he gently kissed the feet of Jesus, who then raised one of His hands, as if imparting a blessing. After this, the other two kings came forward in succession and did likewise.

After each of the three kings had adored Christ in this way, Veronica then heard the kings converse with each other for some time. However, she was unable to comprehend the words which they spoke. The kings then took out from their bags their gifts of gold, frankincense, and myrrh. These they presented to Joseph, to accept on behalf of the infant Jesus. The angel who accompanied Veronica explained into her ear the mystical meaning of these three gifts—namely, gold for His Kingship, frankincense for His Divinity, and myrrh for the terrible bitterness of His passion and death.

Blessed Veronica testified that the three kings were each extremely handsome and of splendid appearance, being robed in garments of cloth-of-gold which fell to their knees. The youngest of the kings, who had adored Christ first, seemed to be most senior of them in terms of gravity and authority. After the three kings, or Magi, had performed their act of worship and homage, they remained in the area for one night only, staying in a nearby inn. Veronica witnessed an angel of the Lord appearing to them, and telling them not to return to Herod, but to commence their homeward journey the next day, traveling by a different route.

After they had departed, the angel who accompanied Veronica then transported her back to the palace of the wicked King Herod. He was boiling over with wrath at the fact that the three kings had not returned to him and cursing with the utmost vehemence all those who were there present. He also promised an immense reward to anyone who could inform him of the whereabouts of the kings or bring them to back to his presence.

It was at this point that Veronica's vision came to an end. She returned to her normal state of mind and found that the other nuns had, by this stage, almost completed the singing of Vespers.[11]

---

[11] Vespers, or evening prayer, is normally celebrated at about 6:00 p.m. This would seem to be several hours after this portion of Blessed Veronica's vision commenced, which was after receiving Holy Communion at the Mass of the day.

5

THE PURIFICATION OF THE BLESSED VIRGIN

On the Solemnity of the Purification of the Blessed Virgin,[12] Blessed Veronica was taken up into mystical ecstasy on two occasions: the first at night before the sun had arisen, and the second at the celebration of the Holy Mass of the feast, after she had received the Most Blessed Sacrament.

In the first of these ecstasies, Veronica beheld celestial wonders and glories which far exceeded the power of human words to describe or portray. In response to a command from the immortal God, she remained silent about these, refusing to try to express that which was inexpressible in human words.

The second of the mystical ecstasies which she experienced on that day was to last for the space of more than three hours. During this second vision, she beheld that she was led into the ancient temple at Jerusalem by an angel. This temple was of an almost miraculous beauty and grandeur. There was a certain,

[12] February 2.

very elderly man there, clad in robes of a dark and somber hue. Next, she saw holy Mary and Saint Joseph, together with the infant Jesus, whom His Mother bore in her arms. Joseph carried with him a pair of turtledoves and two young pigeons, which they placed at the altar.

Next, they approached the old man, to present the Divine Infant to him. Upon seeing the holy child, the old man genuflected in adoration three times, and then took the baby Jesus in his arms. Tears flowed freely from his weary eyes and his face beamed with radiant joy as he kissed the Savior with infinite love and devotion. Then, raising his eyes to heaven, he exclaimed: "Now, O Lord, You may dismiss Your servant in peace, for my eyes have seen Your salvation!" At this point, the angel spoke to Veronica and told her that this was Simeon, the prophet.

Simeon held the Christ-child in his arms for a long period of time, and it seemed to be very difficult for Simeon to be parted from Him when giving the holy infant back to His Mother. He looked upon the face of Jesus, and it seemed to Veronica that the small baby was imparting to him profound mysteries and heavenly truth, by means of the sounds and gestures He made. When he finally handed Jesus back to the Blessed Virgin, he said: "Alas, a sword of sorrow shall pass through your own heart because of this child!"

A very old woman, whom Veronica recognized to be Anna, stood there in the temple as well. Suddenly, inspired by a spirit of prophecy, she gave praise and glory to God and predicted many wonderful and touching things concerning the baby Jesus.

But the words of Simeon, about the sword of sorrow that was destined to pass through her heart, evidently touched Mary very deeply, for her face was shaded with a look of deep melancholy. Jesus Himself, upon perceiving the sadness of His beloved Mother, suddenly appeared also to be saddened. And at that moment, His face was transformed—for though He was but an infant, His expression and countenance changed to that of a man of ancient years, like one who had existed for countless ages and perceived and understood human sorrow to its very depths. And whenever Veronica was to see the face of Jesus again, she realized that there was always a look of infinite compassion and profound gravity upon it, springing from His profound and complete awareness of the sufferings of others.

At this point, Veronica's vision came to an end, and she returned to normal consciousness.

6

THE FLIGHT INTO EGYPT

On the night following the feast of the Epiphany, Blessed Veronica was taken up into a mystical ecstasy. She was led by an angel into a certain house, where the Blessed Virgin and Saint Joseph were both present. She saw that Joseph was sleeping, but she also perceived an angel (a different one from the one who was her companion) appearing to him in a dream. The angel spoke thus to him: "Arise, take the child and His mother, and flee into Egypt! For Herod is infuriated and intent upon killing Him."

Immediately, Saint Joseph arose from his bed. Very quickly, he prepared their donkey, and seated the Virgin and her infant Son upon it. He took with them three maidservants as companions for Mary, together with an ox and three other donkeys and a number of servants to attend to these. The donkeys and ox were laden with provisions for the journey, as well as various domestic necessities. Then they set out promptly, taking a road which led them by a certain forest. All the while, the angel (which was perceived by Joseph and Veronica alone) led him along the way which they were traveling.

Veronica felt herself to be one of the party that accompanied the Holy Family. She seemed to be walking along with them and could see and hear whatever they did or said. The angel who was leading Joseph now led them into the woods. Here, Veronica perceived a great multitude of wild animals of various species come forth. Upon seeing this, the Blessed Virgin was clearly surprised and frightened at first. But then each of the animals lowered itself to the ground before the Christ-child, as if in reverent adoration! When they witnessed this miracle, the whole company were filled with unspeakable joy and wonder.

At times, the Virgin Mary spoke directly to Veronica, as if she were her close companion. And the Mother of God shared with her various divine and heavenly mysteries—making her promise, however, that she would not reveal them to anyone.

How often was Veronica's compassionate heart touched to see the Blessed Virgin fatigued from their long travels! How often she saw the Son of God and the Mother of God both afflicted by the severity of the heat of the day, or the cold at night, or a lack of adequate food and water. At one time, in the middle of the day as they passed through a desert region, she saw Mary and Jesus seek refuge from the sun's burning rays under a palm tree. But the branches of the tree were too small to provide any shade for them. But then, at the nod of the infant Christ, they suddenly grew forth in verdant profusion, as if eager to serve their Lord and His Mother by sheltering them from the cruel sun.

And not only this, but the ground nearby suddenly opened up, and cool and crystal-clear water flowed forth in abundance! It was sufficient not only to quench their desperate thirst, but it allowed them also to refill the various water jars they had taken with them for their journey. That night, as the holy infant slept, Mary was able to spare some of their precious water supplies to wash tenderly the limbs of her Son from the dust of the desert.

Many other times, Veronica saw Mary asking Joseph if they could stop for a while to rest under the shade of some tree. And Joseph always agreed, obeying her with infinite kindness and patience.

After this, Veronica's mind returned from her trance, and she was restored to her usual senses. But she was extremely fatigued in both body and mind, as if she really had undertaken a long journey. Yet all of this journey which she had perceived in her vision, which would have taken many weeks, really only occurred in the space of a single night for Veronica.

The next day, Veronica experienced a continuation of the same vision. This time, she was walking beside the donkey which bore Mary and the infant Jesus. The angel who accompanied her was also there. Both Mary and the angel told her many wondrous things, but Veronica did not disclose them because of the promise of secrecy she had made. Nevertheless, she did retain them in her heart always the words which the Queen of Heaven had spoken to her, and she was filled with ineffable joy whenever she thought of them.

As the journey to Egypt continued, Blessed Veronica saw the Holy Family and their companions to be attacked by a party of bandits. Yet a truly miraculous thing happened then. For a multitude of fierce animals of various species suddenly appeared from their hiding places in the wilderness and attacked the bandits! These thieves then fled in horror, most of them climbing trees to safety. But there was a single one who did not escape. The animals did not tear him apart, but left him cowering in fear, alone and unarmed. But Joseph bravely and kindly approached him, and Joseph treated him kindly as if he were a guest. He similarly called out to the other bandits who had climbed trees, offering them a promise of safety and hospitality, if they, for their part, would solemnly pledge to do no harm to Jesus or Mary.

At this point, the vision of Veronica ended, and she came back to her normal consciousness. Although, as has been mentioned, she did not share the various divine mysteries revealed to her by the Blessed Virgin, she was permitted to relate the following words which Mary spoke to her: "You see—O Veronica, my beloved daughter—all of the duress, hardships and perils I have endured on this journey! Yet I am to sustain much greater sorrows and anxieties in the future. Know this, my sweet and devout daughter, it is impossible to obtain any grace from God unless one experiences sufferings of mind, heart, and body, and works fervently and earnestly to fulfill His holy will."

7

THE LOSS OF JESUS WHEN HE WAS TWELVE YEARS OLD

At the third hour of the night before Sunday,[13] at the Office of Vigils, the Gospel was being read, narrating the loss of Jesus when he was twelve years old. At this point, Blessed Veronica entered a mystical state in which she remained until about midnight. She was taken by an angel to a house in Jerusalem where Mary and Joseph were staying, for they were soon to be departing from that holy city after their annual pilgrimage there.

Now, Mary had been assuming that Jesus was with Joseph, and she was surprised to find that He was not there. A look of concern came across her face, and she spoke into the ears of her earthly spouse: "Oh, where is my Son?"

Joseph replied: "I don't know! I thought that He was with you."

Then both of them began to sigh, casting their eyes about to see if Jesus was anywhere to be found. Then they discussed

---

[13] About 9:00 p.m.

the matter and came to the conclusion that Jesus was probably among their relatives and companions with whom they had made the pilgrimage. So, they decided to make inquiries, for they knew that they were due to make their departure soon.

The Blessed Virgin firstly went to the house where her kinswoman Elizabeth and her husband, Zachariah, were staying. Elizabeth saw that Mary was tearful and upset, and said to her (speaking prophetically, as she had done when Mary visited her during her pregnancy over twelve years before): "O Mary, have you lost your Son?" To this, the Mother of God replied that she had indeed lost Him. Elizabeth then told her that Jesus was not with them, but that she would accompany Mary as she made further inquiries.

So, the two of them, Mary and Elizabeth, went forth to seek Jesus. Next, they went to the house of Anna, the mother of the Blessed Virgin and the grandmother of Christ. After finding that He was not there, Anna also offered to join them as they continued their search.

Filled with tears and anxiety, they continued to inquire among all their relatives and friends. As their search continued without result, the anguish and sorrow of the Blessed Mother steadily increased, until she seemed barely able to sustain herself.

Meanwhile, Saint Joseph was also visiting various places where he knew his kinsfolk and companions were staying. Although the soul of Veronica, being led by her angel guide, had accompanied Mary, Elizabeth, and Anna as they sought the holy Child, she was also able to perceive in her mind the actions of Joseph as he diligently and earnestly sought the young Christ.

Blessed Veronica then returned to her usual senses, as this part of her vision came to an end. She wept bitterly and felt that her heart would almost break as she thought of the great maternal anxiety felt by the Blessed Virgin at that time as she sought after her beloved Son. For most of the day which followed, Veronica continued to weep profusely as if she were a veritable fountain of tears, and she also experienced violent blows from an invisible demon (which afflicted her from time to time). As she lay on her bed, it seemed almost as if there was scarcely a breath of life within her.

But, later that day, Veronica was taken up again into a mystical ecstasy, and her vision continued. This time, her companion angel led her into the square of the Temple of Solomon. A great multitude of people were assembled there, and she heard a certain man speaking to them. He said: "This is indeed an astonishing thing we have witnessed today! For a single Child—a young boy—has disputed with all the experts in the Law and got the better of them. His questions have so confounded and confused them, that these learned men have been left speechless and bewildered, as if they were unlettered simpletons!"

Upon hearing these words, the Blessed Mother of God approached the man who had spoken and asked him for further details of this remarkable Child he had seen. After the man had described Him, she realized it was Jesus, and exclaimed joyfully: "This is my beloved Son, disputing in the temple!"

So, she entered the building of the temple itself, and saw Jesus there. He was seated in a high place, as if upon a throne of judgment. The experts on the Law were all seated around him, listening in rapt attention. But when Jesus saw His Blessed Mother enter, He arose at once and made a sign of love and veneration towards her.

After this, He resumed His seat, and continued His discourse and discussions with the temple authorities. At the conclusion of this, He approached the Blessed Virgin, bowing His head in reverent veneration. Mary embraced Him lovingly and kissed Him tenderly. But, seizing His right hand firmly, she spoke to Him also in words of concerned, maternal reproach: "My Son, why have you done this to us? For Joseph and myself have been searching for you desperately, filled with worry about what had become of You!"

He responded gently: "Why are you searching for Me, My dear Mother? Did you not realize that it behooved Me to visit My heavenly Father's house?" At this point, the Mother of Jesus took hold of His right hand firmly once more, while Elizabeth took His left hand. They then led the holy boy out from the temple. Situated between the two of them, His joy was plainly visible upon His smiling young face. The whole crowd assembled in the temple also witnessed these events, and marveled very greatly, sharing in the joy of both Mother and Son at their reunion.

For all of their journey homeward, from Jerusalem to Nazareth, Veronica continued to accompany the Holy Family and all their traveling party. In her vision, she was the closest companion to the Blessed Virgin throughout this time. And as they traveled, the Mother of God said to her: "Veronica, my beloved daughter, consider all the sorrows and all the anguish which I suffered during those three days when my dear Son was missing! From this, reflect on how we can attain no grace from God, unless we undergo some suffering of mind, heart, and body. Thus, has it come about in me. For I alone have been granted the very fullness of God's grace; yet is there anyone whose sufferings may be compared to my own sufferings?" As Mary spoke these words to Veronica, the eyes of the boy Jesus rested attentively upon Veronica and shone with the light of tender love.

In due course, the traveling party, which was led by Saint Joseph, arrived safely back at Nazareth. They all rejoiced greatly to be back home, and Veronica could see the young Jesus clapping His hands in happiness.

At this point, the vision of Veronica came to its end, and she returned to her normal consciousness.

8

THE BAPTISM OF THE SAVIOR

As the priest was celebrating the Holy Mass on the Sunday after the Octave of the Epiphany,[14] Blessed Veronica was taken up out of her senses and experienced a mystical vision. She was led by an angel to the banks of the River Jordan. There, she saw Christ standing a amidst a large crowd of people. Saint John the Baptist was there also.

Suddenly, Saint John exclaimed in a resonant voice: "Behold, the Lamb of God! Behold Him who takes away the sins of the world!" And as the Baptist approached the Savior, he threw himself face down to the ground in adoration.

Our Lord then addressed him, saying, "Baptize me, John!"

To this, John responded humbly: "It is I who ought to be baptized by You. Are You really coming to *me* to be baptized?"

The Lord answered: "Let it be thus for the present, for it is befitting that all that propriety demands should be fulfilled."

---

[14] On this Sunday, attention is given to the Baptism of the Lord; although, traditionally, this event is believed to have occurred on the same date as the Adoration of the Magi and the Wedding at Cana (January 6).

Then, with great humility, John continued to refuse three times; each time insisting that he was unworthy to place his hands upon the Lord. But finally, he acquiesced. Jesus then removed His garment, and together they entered the flowing waters of the Jordan. John was clad in a coarse robe of camel's hair and had a leather belt fastened around his waist. With fear and trembling, he poured water over the Savior's sacred head, which then flowed down over His whole body.

Christ remained still amidst the waves of the Jordan as the sacramental waters passed over Him. And Veronica saw the Holy Spirit in the form of a radiant dove of the whiteness of snow, with the glowing cross upon its head. And she heard a voice from on high declaring: "This is My beloved Son, in whom I am well pleased." After hearing this, which was clearly the voice of God the Father, Veronica heard the Holy Spirit, in the form of a dove, speak many words to Christ. Veronica stated that she was able to hear and understand all of the words spoken by the dove, but afterwards was somehow unable to recall or repeat them.

There were present also four angels. These stood upon the banks of the Jordan looking on, and carefully holding the garments of Christ in their hands. Veronica realized that these brilliant angels were visible to her alone, but not the gathered crowd. Indeed, she related that angels were always in attendance with Christ, serving Him diligently, although they were invisible to the eyes of the multitude.

When Jesus ascended from the waters, she saw the four angels dress Him once again in His robes. Then Jesus and Saint John entered the waters once again, and this time Jesus baptized John.

After this, Veronica returned to her normal senses for the remainder of the Mass. With several of the other nuns, they reverently received the most Holy Body of Christ from the hands of the priest.

9

THE WEDDING FEAST AT CANA

Once, while Blessed Veronica was at dinner in her convent's dining room with the other sisters, her soul was taken up by an angel and brought to Cana in Galilee. There, she beheld a splendidly decorated large upper room, in which stood a magnificent table, laden with fine food of every imaginable kind. Christ and His holy Mother stood there, as well as a beautifully dressed bride and a bridegroom, and many other guests.

Before the banquet commenced, Christ was called up to bless the food, which He did by raising His hands in reverent prayer. The assembled guests all joined Him in the singing of the customary psalm, as is the practice in religious communities to this day.[15]

All the multitude then took their places in seats around the table, with the Savior Himself sitting at the head of the table,

---

[15] It is an ancient custom amongst religious communities to chant a short psalm (normally Psalm 115, "*Laudate Dominum, omnes gentes . . .*") before commencing a celebratory feast.

and His most Blessed Mother at His right hand. To the left of Jesus sat the bridegroom, while his bride sat in the next place beside the heavenly Virgin. All the other guests sat down in their due order. Veronica herself, together with her companion angel, humbly selected seats for themselves at the very last place of the table, wishing to mingle unobtrusively with the company.

Blessed Veronica relates that the Savior was robed in vestments of superlative splendor, and that His countenance was radiant with serenity, power, and beauty. His Blessed Mother was wearing a magnificent garment of brilliant and spotless white. The bridegroom and bride both wore garments of rich red.

Veronica observed that there were five servants who diligently attended to the table. Two of them were occupied with carrying in the food, while another two divided and served the varied dishes which were taken in. The fifth served as *architriclinus,* or master-of-the feast. He was engaged primarily in filling and refilling the goblets of the guests with varied fine wines, both red and golden. There were roast and baked meats in abundance, artfully prepared in many styles, as well as conch shells from which varied delicious sauces and condiments were available. Christ Himself was invited to commence the feast with the breaking of the bread, and then all the others followed Him in turn.

After the banquet had continued for quite a long time, the Mother of Jesus spoke to Him, observing that the supplies of wine had been exhausted. Her Son replied to her, saying: "O Woman, what concern is that to Me or to you? For My hour has not yet come."

But Mary immediately spoke to the servants. "Whatever He tells you to do," she said, "that you must do!"

Now, there were six large stone water jars present in the room. Jesus said to the servants: "Fill these with water, and then bring them to the master-of-the-feast!" This was done, and when the master-of-the-feast tasted what was in them, that water had become wine. He did not know whence this wine had come, although the other servants knew perfectly well that a miracle had taken place. The master-of-the-feast was astonished at the fine quality of this wine, which he had never experienced before.

He spoke to the bridegroom, saying: "All people serve the best wine first, and, when the guests have become are drunk, then they bring out the inferior wines. But you have saved the very best wine till last!"

Blessed Veronica testifies that the wine created from water was of an intense rich redness, so dark that it was almost purple.

The dishes which formed the main course were then removed, and then wooden dishes, elaborately and ornately carved, were brought in. These contained a variety of light and sweet dainties and confectionaries, which we call "desserts."

After they had partaken of these, some of the guests then took out musical instruments of various kinds and commenced to play joyfully. The bridegroom took the hand of the bride, and they began to dance, as did many of the other guests. The Savior and His Mother, however, did not dance, but remained sitting in serene dignity. Blessed Veronica attests that this dancing at the wedding feast had nothing disorderly or worldly about it but was rather the manifestation of pure and celestial joys. The face of the Lord, she said, was filled with spiritual delight as He looked on.

Here, the vision of Veronica came to an end, and she returned to her customary senses. But many of her sister nuns asked her to share with them what she had witnessed while in a mystical trance—for, indeed, she was still in the dining room of the convent with all the other nuns while this vision had taken place. Eventually overcome by the insistent requests of her sisters and in obedience to the direction of the Mother-Superior of the convent, Blessed Veronica related to everyone assembled what she had witnessed in her vision. And this filled the whole community with great joy, and this vision of the wedding feast at Cana is frequently retold among the nuns of Blessed Veronica's convent to this very day.

10

THE TEMPTATION OF CHRIST IN THE DESERT

On the first Sunday in Lent,[16] after she had reverently received the most Holy Sacrament of the Body of the Lord, Blessed Veronica's soul was taken up by an angel, and she experienced a vision. She was transported in spirit to an arid desert and was to remain there for the space of some seven hours.

She saw Christ there, all alone, looking pale, gaunt, and hungry, and His clothes were tattered and dusty. From the distance, she then saw another man approaching Him. The angel of the Lord said to her: "The one you see approaching Christ, that is the devil—the wicked and bitter foe of the human race! He has disguised himself as a man." This man (or rather, demon, disguised in human form) appeared to be very old, and had the appearance of a hermit. His form and facial features suggested that he had led a life of great austerity, and his demeanor was

[16] The Gospel reading for this Sunday is the temptation of Christ in the desert.

venerable. Indeed, had Veronica not been warned by the angel, she could have imagined him to be some ancient desert saint or holy hermit!

The old man carried with him a basket filled with stones of various shapes and colors. These he placed on the ground in front of Christ. He spoke and said to Christ: "I see that You are suffering very terribly from hunger, my friend! If You are the Son of God, tell these stones to become bread, and they shall indeed become bread."

But the Lord replied: "Man lives not by bread alone, but by every word which proceeds from the mouth of God."

At this point, the demon abandoned his disguise, so that his real identity became visible. He took hold of Christ and placed Him upon a high place. There, he said to Him: "If you are the Son of God, throw Yourself down from here! For it is written that 'God shall command His angels who will take You in His hands, lest You strike Your foot against a stone.'"

Again, Jesus responded, saying: "It is also written: thou shalt not tempt the Lord thy God!"

The devil, by now frustrated and angry, assumed a different form, even more horrible than before. He took Jesus to an extremely high mountain, and he showed Him there all the kingdoms and empires of the world and their glories and riches. He spoke a third time: "All this that You see, I shall give unto You, if You cast Yourself down before my feet and worship me!"

At this point, the devil had taken on a yet more hideous and ghastly aspect, breathing forth acrid flames from his nostrils and mouth. But Jesus replied to him without fear. "Get thee gone, Satan! For it is written: the Lord thy God thou shalt adore, and Him alone shalt thou serve." Then the devil gave forth a dissonant and horrible roar, so loud that the mountain itself shook and seemed about to tumble down.

But at that moment, a great assembly of holy angels appeared, surrounding the Savior with radiant light, and leading Him to a place of miraculous beauty and tranquility. What that place was, Veronica has never been able to say. The angels carefully removed Christ's tattered garments, and replaced them with robes of indescribable splendor, which seemed to be a manifestation of the glory of His divine majesty. And they sang to Him an ineffable hymn of praise, which endless words could never suffice to describe. A table was also prepared for Him by the angels, and Veronica saw these celestial beings serving Him dishes of heavenly food, having within it all sweetness and delight, on plates of glistening gold.

At this point, Christ spoke to Blessed Veronica at some length, revealing wondrous mysteries to her. After this, her vision came to an end, and she returned to her normal corporeal senses.

11

VARIOUS DEEDS OF THE SAVIOR

We judge that several other events which Blessed Veronica witnessed in her visions may be passed over in silence in this record. These are cases where her visions revealed nothing beyond what is openly stated by the four Evangelists. The events she witnessed include the Transfiguration of the Savior on Mount Tabor, healing of various blind persons, the raising of Lazarus from the dead, and many other incidents and miracles.

12

THE CONVERSION OF MARY MAGDALENE AND OTHERS

On the Thursday before Palm Sunday, Blessed Veronica entered into a state of mystical trance. While she was in this state, she was led to a certain place where Christ was present and addressing a crowd. Veronica noticed that He was telling them the parable of the servants who were entrusted with different quantities of money, or different numbers of talents, by their master.

The crowd of people who were present was sizeable, and it included both men and women. But there was one woman who stood out from the rest, and whose presence was conspicuous among the multitude of those listening. She was seated on a higher seat, and was outfitted in an elaborate and ostentatious way, in both her dress and jewelry. Her eyes were restless, and she was constantly moving her head, now looking in one direction, now in another. Her expression was bold, conceited, and shameless.

At the end of the familiar parable of the talents, the Savior looked directly at this woman and exclaimed: "O, poor soul burdened with numberless sins! The talent which *you* have received from the Lord, you have buried in the foulness of the earth. But I tell you, if you leave behind your crimes and your life of sin and debauchery and willingly turn towards Me, I shall receive you with mercy!"

The flamboyantly dressed woman, whom Veronica recognized to be Mary Magdalene, seemed to be utterly unmoved by these words. She stared at Christ with a bold and hard expression which was also vaguely flirtatious, as if expecting to overcome Him by her own force of will, self-confidence, and beauty. Yet Jesus continued to return her look, with manly constancy and unwavering determination. Yet, in His eyes there also shone forth tender love and compassion, as well as invincible fortitude.

Eventually, the woman was overcome, and her self-assurance all vanished. She fell to the ground suddenly, and penitent tears flowed profusely from her previously bold eyes. One by one, she removed her items of showy and expensive jewelry, humbly placing them on the ground. Her sister Martha, who had been standing by quietly and modestly in the background, came forward discreetly and collected these.[17] Finally, Mary Magdalene undid the elaborate braids in which her hair was arranged, and her hair fell in simplicity to her chest. She spoke no word, but

[17] According to ancient tradition of the Church, Saint Mary Magdalene and Saint Martha were sisters.

the sighs and tears of heartfelt repentance and compunction which broke from her audibly spoke more powerfully than any oration or plea.

At the end of His discourse to the crowd, Jesus departed, as if exhausted from having completed a work of strenuous labor. As He was departing, a certain man, known as Simon the Leper,[18] quietly invited Him to his own house for lunch and rest. The Lord gratefully nodded in agreement to this kind invitation, and together they entered Simon's house.

Blessed Veronica saw that Mary Magdalene herself, assisted and comforted by her sister Martha, returned to their own house after the crowd had dispersed. Led by her companion angel, Veronica accompanied these two sisters, and witnessed Mary Magdalene enclose herself in her private chamber. There, she continued to weep bitterly over her past sins for some time. Veronica perceived Martha also, as she went about the domestic duties of the house, aided by their maidservant Marcella, diligently and tenderly ensuring that her sister Mary was well taken care of in her time of sorrow.

Mary Magdalene then found out that Jesus had gone to the house of Simon the Leper for lunch. At once, she took a vessel of her most precious ointment, and hurried to the house of

---

[18] The description of him as "Simon the Leper" clearly does not indicate that he suffered from the contagious skin disease known as leprosy, as this would have prevented him from being present with the crowd. It may have been that he had some other chronic skin condition, such as dermatitis, which gave rise to this cognomen. In the Gospel of Luke, he is referred to simply as "Simon the Pharisee."

Simon, rushing straight in. Veronica saw how Christ was seated there, clearly very fatigued. She saw also Mary Magdalene fall to her knees to anoint Him. The repentant woman flooded His feet with a seemingly endless flow of tears, all the while wiping them with her disheveled but still beautiful hair. And as she did this, she confessed all the sins which had marred her previous life. Her tears flowed in such profusion that it seemed to Veronica to be a veritable river! Veronica also related that the crimes and sins which Mary Magdalene confessed were of a very grave and shameful character, yet she accused herself of them with perfect openness and honesty, in the hearing not only of Christ, but of all there present.

After all of this, Mary began to speak of her sister Martha, saying, "I am indeed blessed to have such a good sister as Martha! How long and hard did she work to rescue me from my sinful way of life! And how often did I arrogantly tell her: 'You can live as you please but let me live as I please! *You* can follow this new prophet whom they call the Christ; but as for me, I will do whatever my inclinations impel me to do!'"

Then, Mary Magdalene addressed herself to Jesus once more. She said: "But You, O Lord and Father of all mercies—I now beg You to forgive me all my many and horrendous sins. Have mercy on me! For far too long have I spurned the just reproaches and corrections of my good sister, Martha, and preferred to wallow in the misery of my wretched iniquity."

For a while, Jesus remained silent, looking upon the weeping woman with a grave but compassionate face. Meanwhile,

Simon the Leper, his host, also looked at her, but with an expression of judgmental pride and contemptuous condemnation. Then Christ spoke to him, telling him the parable of the two debtors—the one of who was forgiven a great debt and so loved much, and the one who had been forgiven but little and so loved very little in return.

Then He spoke to Mary Magdalene, saying: "Your sins are forgiven you, my daughter. Go forth in peace." Immediately, she arose from the ground, blessing the Savior with joyous gratitude. Judging herself to be unworthy of such noble mercy, she was completely overcome with tears of relief and emotion.

At this point, Veronica perceived the home of Mary and Martha again. Martha was there, and upon discovering that Mary had left for the house of Simon the Leper, she herself rushed there after her. When she found her sister weeping, she rejoiced greatly, for she knew that she had also become a disciple of Christ, the true Savior of the world. She knew that her wayward sister had been saved by Him from the dark depths of sin and perdition into which she had hitherto been immersed.

At this point, Blessed Veronica's angel ordered her to return to her normal, waking consciousness. This she did, and so the vision came to its end.

13

THE ENTRY OF CHRIST INTO JERUSALEM ON PALM SUNDAY

On the night before Palm Sunday, an angel of the Lord took Blessed Veronica to the city of Jerusalem in a vision. There, she beheld Christ seated upon a donkey. She noticed that the robes of His disciples had been arranged upon the back of the animal, in the manner of a saddle. The donkey upon which Our Lord rode was surrounded by a considerable retinue of female disciples, including the Blessed Virgin, Saint Martha and Saint Mary Magdalene, and many other faithful women. A vast crowd, consisting not only of the whole populace of the city but also many people from other lands, was gathered. These all looked on with great expectation to see the triumphant entry of the long-awaited Messiah, the foretold King of kings, coming to the city of the temple, humble and mounted upon a donkey.

But Jesus Himself exhibited an aspect of deep melancholy, and tears flowed gently down His face. "Alas!" He said. "Jerusalem,

Jerusalem, if you knew what I know, you too would weep." The most holy Mother of Christ also wept, her own heart being touched with maternal sympathy at seeing her beloved Son crying in this way. All the women who accompanied Christ, walking in procession around the donkey He rode, also mourned and lamented—and especially Mary Magdalene, whose tears flowed more freely and profusely than anyone else, aside from the Blessed Virgin herself.

The angel who accompanied Blessed Veronica then pointed out to her that the great multitude did not all exhibit the same emotions. Although all were filled with interest to see the entry of the Lord into Jerusalem, there were some who rejoiced with exultant jubilation. These were primarily foreigners, such as Greeks and Romans, Samaritans, and Galileans. But there were others those who looked on with bitterness and resentment, including the Jewish elders, Pharisees, Sadducees, and Herodians.[19]

She observed that it was Hebrew boys who were carrying branches of various trees, including olive trees and palms, and casting their vestments on the ground before the Lord. They cried out in joyful acclamation: "Blessed is He who comes in

---

[19] Here, the wording of the original is: "*Populus hic, quem gaudiis affectum intueris, populus est gentium, alter tristes vultus pre se ferens Hebraeus existit.*" But since, in the very next sentence, Veronica described Hebrew boys as applauding Christ, it seems reasonable to assume that by "*populus Hebraeus,*" she means specifically the Jewish elders, Pharisees, etc. The translation offered is intended to convey this sense.

the name of the Lord!" Veronica testified that the branches of the palms and the olives that were being carried spontaneously bent themselves down as Christ passed by, as if in veneration. However, the branches of the reeds, unlike the other branches, refused to do so.[20] Veronica noticed also that the great multitude of boys waving branches were all about the same age, and it was revealed to her that they were all twelve years old. The angel secretly explained to Veronica the symbolic meaning of all of this.[21]

When the Savior arrived at the square before the temple, He descended from His donkey, assisted by His disciples. Then, moving to an elevated place within the temple, He addressed the crowd in fervent words of wisdom and hope. At the end of His address, Jesus seemed to be fatigued and was perspiring profusely.

Immediately, Martha, ever diligent and attentive, realized that Christ had consumed no food that day, and that no one had yet invited Him to take refreshment and rest at their home. The Spirit seemed to impel her forcefully, and she rushed through the middle of the crowd and invited the Lord, together with His closest disciples, to come to her house. The Savior

---

[20] This interesting observation reflects a prevalent Medieval folk-belief or tradition. It is possibly connected with the fact that it is specified that Christ was later to be struck with reeds, and so the reeds were considered to be among the 'persecutors' of Christ.

[21] This secret symbolic meaning is not given here. It is possible that it was revealed to Blessed Veronica with instructions that she not share it with anyone else.

graciously and thankfully accepted this invitation. Martha then immediately rushed home in order to prepare a meal, which she did with the assistance of her maidservant, Marcella.

Meanwhile, the angel of the Lord who was the companion of Blessed Veronica told her that she needed to return to her normal senses at this time. And so, her vision ended. It was then the middle of the day of Palm Sunday. Midday prayer was sung, and then Veronica, together with the other sisters of her convent, went in together to the dining room. Until then, no one had eaten anything, due to the fasting requirements of that day. Veronica ate lightly, and then returned to her room to pray privately.

Again, she was taken up into a mystical trance, and her vision continued. This time, the angel of the Lord led her to the house of Martha. There, she saw the Savior seated with His disciples. The Lord was blessing the food which had been set before them. His Blessed Mother was present as well. She sat at His right, followed by Mary the mother of James, and Salome, and a number of other devout women. To His left sat the apostle Saint John. Mary Magdalene meanwhile was at His feet, listening attentively to His words and gazing upon His divine countenance in rapt contemplation.

Veronica attests that the food which was served was extremely fine and varied. Nevertheless, she noticed that meat and dairy products were entirely absent, consistent with the practice of the Catholic Church during Lent.

Martha spoke to Jesus, saying: "Lord, do You not care that my sister has left me to do all the serving myself? Please, tell her to help me!" To this, Christ responded with a happy face: "Martha, Martha, you are anxious, and concerned for many things! But Mary has chosen the better part, and it shall not be taken from her."

Martha accepted these words of the Lord with great happiness and serenity, and she rejoiced that her sister Mary was given this privileged gift of contemplation by God.

When Christ had completed His meal, all of those present gave gracious thanks to God, led by the Savior. The Savior then spoke to Veronica, urging her to share all that she had witnessed in this vision with her fellow nuns. She noticed also that it was only after Jesus had finished His meal that the other disciples began to eat—with the single exception of John, the beloved disciple, who had eaten along with the Lord.

14

THE FINAL SUPPER TOGETHER OF JESUS AND MARY

On the night of the Lord's Supper, Blessed Veronica was taken up into a mystical trance and led by an angel to Bethany, into the house of Martha and Mary Magdalene. There, she saw a table in an upper room, at which were seated Christ and the Blessed Virgin. No one else was present, so that they were able to speak with each other in perfect privacy. The divine Son and the Blessed Mother spoke freely of the passion which Christ was to undergo. Jesus urged Mary to endure with patience all the great sufferings of soul and heart which He knew lay in store for her. He also warned her not to fall prey to despair at His impending death.

"For it is necessary for Me to go forth to Jerusalem now," Jesus said, "to have my Last Supper with my disciples there, and to undergo death upon the cross."

Upon hearing these fateful words, the merciful Mother gave forth deep sighs from the depths of her heart, and burning tears flowed forth from her eyes. She urged her Son not to undertake this journey to Jerusalem. But Christ expounded to her the ancient oracles of the prophets which foretold the inevitability and necessity of the only-begotten Messiah of God, and His duty of obedience to the will of the eternal Father. He explained that it was to fulfill this very destiny that He had come into the world, in order to save the human race from sin and eternal damnation.

Blessed Veronica witnessed the holy Mother of God hear these words attentively and ponder them deeply. Yet although the Blessed Virgin understood all these things, the maternal anxiety and compassion she felt seemed to overwhelm her, and she almost collapsed to the ground. But Christ was at hand to raise her up gently and lovingly.

The Mother and Son spent the whole night in private colloquy, exchanging words of infinite love and divine wisdom. So intent were they upon their conversation that neither of them consumed any food. At the end of this night-long exchange, Veronica saw Jesus and Mary rise from the table. Jesus then knelt reverently before Mary and requested her maternal blessing for the ordeal which lay ahead of Him. Then the Blessed Virgin knelt before her Son and requested His blessing, for she knew that this Son of hers was truly God Himself. With tears of love, they exchanged blessings in this manner.

After this, Mary, with natural maternal love, urged Him to remain with her longer. "My Son, do not depart from me!" she exclaimed, her voice ringing out with such dolorous passion that everyone in the house could hear her clearly. Mary Magdalene quickly rushed in, inflamed with the fire of love, and anxiously asked the Mother of Christ what was the cause of her plaintive exclamation and the tears which she shed in such profusion. The Blessed Virgin replied: "Ask this of my Son! For He has resolved to go forth to Jerusalem, where it is certain that He will undergo most dire sufferings and a terrible death."

Upon hearing these words, Mary Magdalene threw herself at the feet of Jesus. With tears of tender love, she implored Him: "My Master, do not go to Jerusalem, I beg You! For You know full well all the wicked and diabolical plans which the temple authorities have contrived against You."

But to this, Christ replied firmly: "Do not ask me such a thing! For it is the divine plan that I go forth to the Holy City at this time, and there I am destined to undergo much suffering and death."

Blessed Veronica observed Jesus remain in the presence of the two women for a little longer, and then He departed quietly. At this point, His Mother spoke to Mary Magdalene, saying: "O Mary Magdalene, follow my Son! Hasten after Him, and in my own name, implore Him to return to me!" And Mary Magdalene did just as the holy Mother of God had instructed her, and soon conveyed these words of maternal pleading to Jesus. But He ordered this most devoted of His disciples to return quickly to His Mother, and to solemnly assure Her that very soon He would indeed return joyfully to her presence in the near future—but only after He had fulfilled His divinely preordained destiny of suffering, dying, and rising again from the tomb, for the salvation of all mankind.

Mary Magdalene returned to the Virgin Mary and told her everything that her Son had said. Blessed Veronica testified that she witnessed tears and laments of almost indescribable sorrow and anguish then to come forth from both the Mother of Christ and Saint Mary Magdalene. Though they both had absolute faith in the promise of the glories of the Resurrection, yet they were horrified at the thought of the agonies and shame which Jesus, whom they each loved dearly, was to undergo. And so, they gave free rein to all the bitter heartbreak they shared at that time.

Veronica was also granted a vision of the face of Christ at that time. She noticed that it was suddenly imbued with a deathlike pallor and bore an expression of genuine human dread and foreboding which He never once displayed before His disciples or the public. Indeed, it almost seemed to become, for an instant, the face of another person altogether . . .

15

THE LAST SUPPER

After Blessed Veronica had witnessed in her vision that final supper of Jesus and Mary, and the events which followed it, she was next transported by her companion angel to Jerusalem, to the time and place of the Last Supper of the Lord with His disciples. Jesus was now in Jerusalem, although it was just a moment before (in her vision, at least) that Veronica had seen Him depart from the house of Saint Martha and Saint Mary Magdalene.[22]

Veronica firstly saw Christ addressing His disciples, saying to them: "Go forth and organize everything, so that we may celebrate the Passover meal together. As you enter the city, you will come across a certain man carrying a jar of water. Follow him into whatever house he enters. Then say to the master of that house that the Master says to him: 'Where is the chamber in which I may eat the Passover with my disciplines?' He will then show you a large upper room. Prepare there all that is necessary."

---

[22] In Bethany.

Veronica attested that she then saw all of this happening, noticing that the jar of water which the man was carrying was of exceptional beauty. She saw the disciples preparing everything in the upper room, and then Christ joining them to consume the Passover. The disciples all bore looks of sadness as they heard the Savior speak to them of many new and perplexing things. And though they listened attentively, they could fully comprehend very little of what He said to them.

After the Passover meal had come to its conclusion, Jesus arose from the table. Removing His garments, He clad Himself in white linen. Pouring some water into a basin, He then began to wash the feet of His disciples, wiping them dry with the linen cloth with which He had vested Himself.

But when He came to Simon Peter, Peter said to Him: "Lord, are you going to wash *my* feet?" And the conversation which followed was exactly that which is narrated by the Evangelist Saint John.[23] After He had washed the feet of each one of them, Jesus then tenderly and humbly kissed their feet.

Blessed Veronica described the upper room in which the Last Supper took place as being extraordinarily beautiful and ornate. The table was rectangular and elevated only slightly from the floor. It was on the left side of the upper room that the basin and linen with which the Savior washed the feet of His disciples were positioned.

After the washing of the feet was completed, Jesus again vested Himself in His regular garments. Then He resumed His

---

23 See John 13.

seat at the table at which the disciples sat. He took bread, blessed it, broke it, and gave it to his disciples, saying: "Take this, all of you, and eat of it. This is My Body." Then, in a similar way, He took the chalice, saying: "Take this, all of you, and drink from it. For this is the chalice of My Blood, the Blood of the new and eternal covenant!"[24]

Then Christ said to the gathered disciples: "Amen, amen, I say to you that one of you shall betray me!" Upon hearing this, the disciples exchanged looks with each other in a confused and concerned manner. Indeed, they were all astonished, and many of them began to shed tears upon hearing of this impending acting of perfidious treachery, which one of their own number was to commit. Blessed Veronica attested that she could hear each and every word that the Savior spoke at that time, and also what the various disciples said among themselves.

After Jesus had finished speaking to them of the mysteries of the Kingdom of God, each one of His disciples approached Him and embraced Him. Together with His disciples, Christ departed from the upper room and went forth into the night.

Blessed Veronica relates how the angel of the Lord who accompanied and guided her then led her out, following the

---

[24] In the Gospel of John, which describes the washing of the feet, the 'Institution Narrative' is not given. In Veronica's vision, the consecration of the bread and wine follows the washing of the feet, and was not part of the actual Passover meal (which preceded the washing) but rather was a separate event following it. Veronica's vision seems to harmonize the version of John with that of the synoptic Gospels.

footsteps of the Savior. Jesus and His disciples crossed the Kidron River and came to a place where there was a garden and entered into it. Veronica saw Christ on His knees there, in fervent prayer, and also an angel of the Lord who was revealing to Jesus a vision of the suffering which awaited Him.

After Christ had prayed intensely some three times, Judas arrived on the scene, together with a cohort of temple guards. Jesus arose promptly and fearlessly to meet them. "Whom do you seek?" He asked the armed throng. They responded: "Jesus the Nazarene." Our Lord answered simply: "I am He." This dialogue was repeated three times.

It was after this that the cohort arrested Christ, together with the Roman tribune and the servants of the temple authorities. They bound Him with rope as they led Him away.

Veronica attests that this arrest of the Lord was in fact a terrible ordeal. For the servants of the temple authorities gathered around Him, circling like ravenous wolves circle an innocent lamb, hungry for blood. Jesus fell to the ground, and they struck Him repeatedly on the face with their fists. Then they placed a great chain of iron around His neck, dragging Him along by this. All the while, the wicked and diabolic crowd insulted Him with devilish hatred. They struck Him also with the hilts of their swords and hurled rocks at Him.

This continued until they reached the Kidron River. There, they threw Him into the swirling waters, without however, releasing him from the long chain which was affixed around His neck. All the while, they cried out with atrocious and hateful blasphemies, mocking and insulting the one they knew to be the Son of God.

16

THE TRIAL AND SENTENCING OF CHRIST, AND HIS CARRYING THE CROSS TO CALVARY

Once the temple authorities had led Christ into the city of Jerusalem, Blessed Veronica saw Jesus being presented to the high priests, Annas and Caiaphas. And she witnessed all that He suffered before those wicked and corrupt judges.

Regarding the man who is described in the Gospel as having slapped Christ in the face,[25] Veronica attests that he wore a gauntlet of iron upon the hand with which he struck the Lord. Such was the force of the blow and the sharpness of the edges of the gauntlet he wore, that blood flowed from Christ's face, staining His neck and His beard. And when He was tied to a pillar of wood and scourged by the Jews, a veritable rain of blood poured from His most sacred body. Then they twisted a crown of thorns and placed it upon His sacred head and robed

[25] See Jn 18:22.

Him in purple. This purple robe, however, was filthy and ugly, and almost frayed to shreds, and so of thoroughly disgraceful appearance.

His tormentors then blindfolded the eyes of Jesus and knelt before Him in mock veneration. Then they spat upon His face. But Jesus, as a meek lamb led to the slaughter, remained perfectly silent, raising no complaint or resistance.

After Pilate had passed the sentence of death on Him, the spirit of Veronica witnessed the assembled crowd, led by the temple authorities, placing the cross upon His holy shoulders. Meanwhile, the air was filled with the grim thunder of the soldiers' weapons clanging, and the blasphemous clamor of the unruly and demon-possessed mob. They all seemed to be in a great hurry to lead Christ to the place of His execution. But, by this time, He was so exhausted and drained from the torments He had endured that He seemed to be only half alive—indeed, it seemed as if His limbs and joints could barely sustain Him upright when the weight of the of the cross was placed upon His heavenly shoulders.

Veronica attests that the chief of the guards led Christ out from Pilate to carry the cross at the hour when the sisters of her convent customarily sung the office of lauds.[26] For this reason, after she experienced this vision, whenever Blessed

---

[26] Lauds, or morning prayer, would normally be done at about the time of sunrise. However, this does not seem consistent with the Gospel narrative of Christ's trial and sentencing. It may well have been that the nuns at Blessed Veronica's convent celebrated lauds a little later in the morning.

Veronica heard the bell for lauds to be sounded in her convent, she would be filled with grievous sadness as she recollected what her beloved Jesus had suffered at that same time.

As Christ proceeded out of the city of Jerusalem, bearing the heavy and fateful burden of His cross, Veronica perceived His most holy Mother approaching Him. Her expression was that of the most bitter and painful grief, and tears flowed from her eyes in endless streams. She was accompanied by Saint John, Saint Mary Magdalene, and also several other devoted women disciples.

Though the glorious Mother of God and her companions strove to reach her Son, nevertheless the unruly throng of the bloodthirsty crowd prevented them from reaching Him. Then Veronica heard Mary say to John: "I beg of you, O most beloved and faithful disciple of Christ, since you know all the byways of this city so well, to take me by some other path, so that I may be able to reach my Child directly and embrace Him once more before He dies!"

Upon hearing these words from the Blessed Virgin, John led Mary, along with a band of other loyal disciples, through various back alleys and unknown byways. In this way, they managed to reach Christ ahead of the crowd that followed Him. Jesus, perceiving His Mother in front of Him, exclaimed: "O Mother, you are here with Me in the darkest depths of My sorrows!" And they embraced each other lovingly, and exchanged tears and kisses which bespoke of a bond of love stronger and more tender than any human words could ever express. Mary's tears of maternal grief and anguish mixed freely with Christ's own tears of dire pain, fatigue, and gentle compassion.

As Mother and Son embraced thus, the cross suddenly fell from His shoulders. A man who stood by grasped it and supported it, for as long as the tender and dolorous exchange continued. But then the ministers of hell—that is to say, the temple guards—ruthlessly compelled Christ to continue with His journey. But by this stage, the Savior was barely capable of supporting Himself under the huge weight of the wooden instrument of death and torture that He carried. So, the guards seized a bystander, a man named Simon of Cyrene, and directed him to carry the cross.

We have put into brief words the sights witnessed and related to us by the holy virgin, Veronica, concerning all that took place in Jerusalem that day. What she saw, though, in all its horrifying details and heartbreaking vividness, far exceeds that which we have been able to commit here to pen and paper.

17

THE CRUCIFIXION AND DEATH OF CHRIST

After the Savior had arrived at Mount Calvary, driven on by the baleful crowd, His vestments were removed, and He was left naked. And when the only-begotten Son of the Almighty King of the Universe was thus denuded, His wounds all poured forth blood afresh, mixing with the coagulated blood which had already gathered on both His Body and His garments. From His shoulders, it flowed down over His entire form in crimson rivulets descending to His feet. Because of this, there was barely a spot on His whole body that was free from red gore; indeed, it was as if He spoke with the psalmist: "No soundness remains in my flesh!"[27]

The Virgin Mother was present in the midst of the crowd, observing everything with anxious maternal attention, her tears flowing unceasingly. When she saw her Son stripped of His garments, hastily she took the veil from her own head, and

[27] Ps. 37:4 in the Douay-Rheims translation; Ps 38:3 in RSVCE.

threw it to Him. Jesus received this gratefully and girded His loins with it.

Blessed Veronica attests that the cross on which the Savior was to die was of great weight and size, and it was placed on the ground beside Him. He was then placed upon it, with arms extended. His diabolical adversaries "encircled Him like many dogs, or like or fat oxen opening their mouths over Him."[28]

The executioners then seized the nails and attempted to extend His hands and feet to the places on the cross where the holes had been bored. But they found that they were unable to stretch out His arms and legs far enough to reach them. So, they affixed rope to His arms and legs firmly, and used this to stretch Him by brute force, so that all of His joints were dislocated. Indeed, His shoulders were pulled out of their natural position in their sockets in order to stretch out His arms so that His hands could reach the holes.

When this was done, the first nail was driven through His right hand, and the second through His left hand. As they were hammered in, the blows rang out thunderously and sickeningly, as if the hammer were being struck directly and forcefully on hard wood. The same procedure was then done with each of His feet, so that the body of the Savior was agonizingly stretched and distorted beyond the bounds of nature.

When this was all completed, the servants of Satan—that is, the executioners of Christ—raised up the cross bearing the

---

[28] See Ps. 21:13, 17 in the Douay-Rheims translation; Ps 22:12–13, 16 in RSVCE.

Sacred Body of God, with bestial and unheard-of cruelty. They did this so that all onlookers could view more easily the unspeakable pains and torments which Jesus endured.

The cruelty of the executioners was witnessed by Blessed Veronica very clearly and closely. After they had raised up the cross the first time, they deliberately let it fall to the ground, and then lifted it up again. Needless to say, this increased the pains of Christ beyond all comprehension. They also deliberately swayed the cross from right to left, which caused the sacred wounds of the Lord to be opened yet more broadly, in agonizing fashion.

When Jesus was so cruelly affixed to the cross, His Virgin Mother beheld the bruised and bloody Body of her beloved Son. In a voice of the most poignant lamentation, she exclaimed: "Alas, alas! O my precious Son, the horrors which You foretold have indeed come to pass. Now has come the dreaded time of which You so often spoke—the time when I would see Your sufferings yet be unable to embrace You! Now the terrible oracle which Simeon uttered all those years ago is fulfilled. For he said that a sword of sorrow would pass through my heart on account of You. O my sweetest Son, truly this moment is for me the sharpest of swords, the cruelest of daggers, which cuts through both my heart and my soul—for I see You, my beloved, hanging in agony and shame from this cross!"

The most Blessed Mother continued thus for some time, often falling to the ground from the very intensity of her affliction. When this happened, Saint Mary Magdalene would gently raise her up, assisted by the other devout women who accompanied her.

Blessed Veronica relates that, guided by her angel companion, she witnessed each and every movement of Christ upon the cross. The crown of thorns pierced Him cruelly, for, as He hung suspended from the cross, He had literally "nowhere to rest His head,"[29] which bowed limply to His chest whenever the strength of His neck failed.

When Christ said, "I thirst," His Blessed Mother exclaimed: "O my Son, once I nursed You at my bosom, but now I am unable to offer You anything to quench Your thirst!" And as she said these words, she fainted to the earth, completely overcome with heartbreak.

In spirit, Veronica perceived Christ to be transformed as the hour of His death approached. Tears flowed continuously down His cheeks, but He uttered not a single word or sound beyond those recorded by the holy Evangelists. As Mary also saw that the death of her Son was now very nigh, she drew even closer to the cross, and cried out: "O my Son, I see You now dying. Do You have any final words of instructions for Your faithful and loving Mother?"

Christ looked upon her and then cast His eyes towards John, who was the only one of the apostles to remain standing faithfully by Him. He said: "Woman, behold your son." Then, turning to John, He said, "Son, behold your Mother." Then,

---

[29] Mt 8:20.

amidst her freely flowing tears, Mary exclaimed: "Now I know, O my Son, that You have appointed me as Mother of all Your disciples. You have given me John as a son, yet am I about to lose my true and divine Son. Alas for this most sorrowful exchange!"

At this point, the face of Jesus, the Son of the omnipotent King, was suddenly cast over with a ghostly pallor, while His eyes grew dim with the shadow of death. Then, in a great voice, He exclaimed: "It is consummated!" And He gave up His spirit. . . .

18

THE MIRACLES WHICH OCCURRED AT THE DEATH OF CHRIST, AND HIS BURIAL

Once the Savior had died, the Blessed Virgin Mother fell to the earth and seemed to cling to it, as if longing for it to swallow her up. It was only with some difficulty that the other women disciples were able to restore her to consciousness and raise her to her feet.

Blessed Veronica related that at the moment at which Christ gave up His spirit to the Father, she witnessed the sun being eclipsed with darkness, rocks being split asunder, tombs springing open, and a powerful and awesome earthquake shaking the ground. She saw also many fleeing from the scene, striking their chests in sincere and overwhelming penitence.

She perceived the centurion, Longinus, opening the side of the Savior with a lance, and blood and water flowing forth freely from the resultant sacred wound. She saw also that when this occurred, this same Longinus was converted to faith in Christ, and his vision was miraculously restored to him, for he had been blind until that point.[30]

But when the centurion Longinus pierced the side of Christ, Veronica saw Mary also again overwhelmed with sorrow, as she collapsed to the ground in grief once more. She relates that everyone departed from the scene at this point, with the exception of the Blessed Virgin, Saint John, Mary Magdalene, and a few other faithful women disciples. Blessed Veronica herself, accompanied by her companion angel, was among the company of these holy women disciples.

All of the company wept and lamented as they gazed upon the pallid and yet still beautiful face of Jesus. They desired also to remove His lifeless body from the cross from which it was still suspended but were unable to do so. At this point, Joseph [of Arimathea] and Nicodemus arrived on the scene. Upon seeing them approaching, Mary's face was first filled with fear; but when she recognized them to be disciples and sympathizers of Her Son, she was immediately relieved. Both were robed in black garments of mourning. Firstly, they knelt before the Blessed Virgin in profound veneration and love, and then they bowed before Saint John in reverence and respect. With touching sincerity, they offered their condolences to both the Mother

---

[30] This is in accordance with ancient traditions concerning the centurion who opened the side of Christ with a lance. According to such traditions, he was called Longinus and was blind (hence his being assigned to relatively undemanding guarding and supervisory duties). When he pierced the side of Christ, he was converted to belief and his sight was also miraculously restored to him. He is generally regarded as being the same centurion who declared, "Truly, this man was the Son of God" (Mt 27:54).

of God and the beloved disciple, for they sensed the pain which afflicted them both at this time—and, to a more moderate degree, shared in it themselves.

Next, they both prostrated themselves before the cross of the Savior in adoration and gazed upon His sacred Body in the worship of silent contemplation, as burning tears welled up in their eyes. Then, ascending by means of ladders, they removed the nails and took down the lifeless body of Christ, placing it respectfully in the tender embrace of His most Holy Mother.

As Mary received the body of her Son, she broke out in tears again, as if another sword of sorrow had passed through her heart. She exclaimed passionately three times: "O, my Son!" Such was the poignancy of her utterances that everyone who heard her was themselves moved to fresh tears. But the lament of the Virgin surpassed that of all others in intensity, purity, and touching beauty.

After this, the body of Jesus was positioned in the tomb, and a large boulder was placed over its entrance. The Blessed Mother of Christ resisted the initial attempts to take her Son's body from her arms; yet, at the firm command of Saint John, she finally consented to release Him from her embrace. Then John led Mary, together with some other devout disciples, to a certain house where they took rest, on the side of Mount Zion. All the while, Blessed Veronica, followed by her angel, accompanied them, until they had all retired to rest.

After this, Veronica's angel led her forth to the Temple of Solomon. . . .

19

THE TEMPLE OF SOLOMON AND OTHER VISIONS

Once Blessed Veronica had been taken within the most magnificent Temple of Solomon, her companion angel spoke to her, saying: "This place which you behold in all its splendor and grandeur is the Temple of God raised up by King Solomon!" Veronica testifies that in all her life she never saw any church or temple which could be compared to it in its size, majesty, and beauty. She said that even the magnificent basilica in Milan could not be remotely compared to it. Everywhere there were great columns fashioned from glowing gemstones of enormous size and adorned with carvings of almost unimaginable intricacy and artistry.

After this, the angel led the spirit of Blessed Veronica to purgatory, where the souls of those who had lived before the Incarnation were held captive. She saw the soul of Christ enter that realm in glorious triumph, and all the souls of those who were destined to be redeemed being liberated from their bonds and ascending to the Kingdom of Heaven.

It is to be noted that we have described Veronica's visions of the passion of Christ only very briefly. But in fact, Veronica saw everything which transpired over those three fateful days—Holy Thursday, Good Friday, and Holy Saturday—in full and complete detail. Veronica describes the cruelty and horror of the passion of Christ as being so extreme that no mortal words could every suffice to express it accurately.

After this first revelation of the passion of Christ, Blessed Veronica relates that every Friday for the space of a year, she experienced renewed visions of three particular mysteries—namely, His arrest in the Garden of Gethsemane, His binding to the column, and the piercing of His hands and feet with the nails as He was affixed to the wood of the cross. And, in the month of March of that year,[31] on every Friday of that month, she witnessed a renewed vision of the entire passion of the Savior. She related that Christ had told her that this was because it was on a Friday in that month that He had laid down His life for the salvation of the world. And He wished that His death should always be commemorated on a Friday, rather than on a fixed date every year, and it was His will that this same passion be reverently remembered on each and every Friday of the year.

[31] This would always be in the season of Lent.

20

THE RESURRECTION OF THE LORD

On the day of Easter Sunday, after receiving the most Holy Eucharist, Blessed Veronica was taken up into a mystical rapture, which continued until the hour of lunch. The beginning of this mystical trance, or vision, was witnessed by all the sisters of the convent. This was unusual, as Veronica's visions normally occurred at night when she was alone.

In the course of her trance, Veronica's companion angel led her to Mount Zion, to the house in which the Blessed Virgin had retired, led by Saint John, after the burial of Christ. Saint Mary Magdalene was present as well, and both the Mother of God and this devout female disciple of Jesus were weeping together in sorrow. Then Mary Magdalene asked the Virgin Mary for her permission to depart from her for a while, to go and visit the tomb in which the mortal remains of Jesus had been laid to rest. The Blessed Mother consented to this, and Veronica perceived a certain mysterious look of sudden and almost secret joy pass over her face, as Mary Magdalene went forth to the tomb.

Then Blessed Veronica had a private vision which explained this appearance of secret joy upon the face of the Virgin Mary at this time. For she saw Christ Himself, already risen from the tomb, garbed in a brilliant white garment and radiant with luminous splendor. He entered the house where His Mother was mourning, unseen by anyone except for Mary herself and Blessed Veronica. Mary and Jesus greeted each other with overwhelming joy and embraced tenderly.[32]

After this, the mind of Veronica was led by her companion angel to follow in the footsteps of Mary Magdalene as she set forth for the tomb of Jesus. Everything happened there precisely as the Gospel relates. She saw Christ in the garden near the tomb, having the appearance of a gardener.[33] Then, later, He appeared to two of the disciples, having the appearance of a pilgrim on His way to Emmaus.[34] Blessed Veronica was able to hear everything that Our Lord said, both when He appeared as a gardener and when He appeared as a pilgrim. She then saw Christ appearing to the four women on the day of the Resurrection. The angel also revealed to Veronica the names of each of these four women.[35]

---

32 This earlier appearance of the risen Christ to Mary does not appear in the Gospels, but it should be read as a part of Blessed Veronica's private revelation.

33 See Jn 20:1–9.

34 See Lk 24:13–15.

35 The account of a small number of women who visit the empty tomb and become the first witnesses to the Resurrection is contained in each of the synoptic Gospels. Yet the Gospel accounts contain some ambiguity as to the

After this, Veronica's vision ended, and she returned to her normal senses.

Such was the humility of Veronica that she blushed with modesty when she realized that all of the other sisters had perceived her entering into a mystical trance at this time. But she derived consolation and encouragement from certain words the Savior spoke to her. For He said: "O my daughter, I have granted you this vision as a special gift! But know that there are certain secrets which I still choose to keep from you."

We should not neglect to mention that, for the space of a year, on every Sunday, this vision of the Resurrection of the Lord was renewed in the heart and mind of Veronica. She relates that Christ said to her on several occasions: "O my daughter Veronica, know that I am willing and able to bestow this vision of My Resurrection on whomsoever prays for it with sincerity and fervor. Therefore, I direct you to pray to Me in this way: *O Lord, for the honor of Your most holy Resurrection, grant unto me this gift, if it be Your will, and if it will be useful for the salvation of my soul. Amen.*"

---

names and identities of these women: Matthew 28:1 has "Mary Magdalen and the other Mary," Mark 16:1 gives "Mary Magdalene, Mary the mother of James, and Salome," Luke 24:10 gives "Mary Magdalene, Joanna, and Mary the mother of James," while John identifies only Mary Magdalene. It seems that the angel clarified to Veronica the exact number and names of the women present.

21

THE ASCENSION OF THE LORD

On the night before the Solemnity of the Ascension of the Lord, immediately after the Office of Vigils,[36] Blessed Veronica sought out a secluded place where she could devote herself to prayer until dawn. Almost immediately, her mind was taken up into a mystical ecstasy and, while in this state, she experienced a vision.

She was taken to a large upper room. In this upper room was Christ, now risen from the dead, the Blessed Virgin, and the apostles. She heard Christ announcing to them: "Now is the hour for Me to ascend to My Father!"

Upon hearing this, Veronica perceived that Mary and all of the apostles began to look saddened and downcast. But immediately, the Savior offered them the following words of consolation: "Do not let your hearts be troubled, for I shall not leave You as orphans. Behold, I will be with you always. And I will send you a Comforter—the Holy Spirit—by whom you will be filled with a joy so great that it will exceed all words! Indeed,

[36] Probably sometime between 2:00–3:00 a.m.

unless I depart from you, you will not be able to receive this Holy Spirit."

When He had said this and many other words of encouragement and consolation to them, He was raised up to the heavens. Radiant clouds surrounded Him and concealed Him from their eyes, while a multitude of angels, aflame with celestial splendor, sang His praises in endless streams of transcendent harmonies. As Christ ascended through each of the various orbs of the heavens, new legions of angels greeted Him with heavenly hymns of jubilation and glory. Many of these angels also bore golden thuribles, with which they incensed Him in adoration.

When Jesus entered the very highest heaven—the Heaven of Heavens— in supreme triumph, God the Father and God the Holy Spirit came forth to greet Him, as if in ecstatic contemplation of the Beatific Vision. Christ then assumed His throne at the right hand of the Father. Ineffable and blinding glory suffused and surrounded these three Persons—Father, Son, and Holy Spirit—in a such a manner that they became indistinguishable and inseparable in the immortal splendor of the one God.

This wonderful vision continued for Blessed Veronica until the eleventh hour of the day, as calculated according to the customs of Milan.[37] During this time, the mystical delights which she experienced may only be compared with the eternal and infinite joys of heaven itself.

[37] Probably about 5:00 p.m.

22

THE SENDING OF THE HOLY SPIRIT

On the night before the glorious festivity of the Solemnity of Pentecost, Veronica experienced a splendid and magnificent vision of the celestial kingdom and saw Christ in the very highest realms of the heavens. He was genuflecting in adoration before the unseen Father, saying: "O My most holy Father and eternal Begetter, You know that I have dwelt among mortals and walked upon the earth. And I pledged most solemnly, both to my glorious ever-Virgin Mother and my faithful apostles, that I would send to them the Holy Spirit. Behold, this very day is the time appointed for the sending of this divine Spirit. Therefore, I beseech You, O heavenly Father, to do this great thing, which I have promised!"

To this humble filial supplication, the eternal Father replied, speaking as if from the unfathomable voids of inaccessible light: "My beloved Son, when I declared that all power on heaven and earth had been given over to You, I thereby pledged Myself to send the Holy Spirit, in accordance to Your promise, and to fulfill everything else You may have pledged!"

Upon hearing these awesome words, Blessed Veronica's mystical trance ceased, and she returned to her normal senses. She continued in intense prayer and meditation until the celebration of the holy Mass of the Solemnity, at which she received most reverently the Blessed Sacrament of the Eucharist. Upon returning to her place, she was taken up into mystical rapture once more, and her vision was renewed.

She was led by an angel into a large upper room, in which were the holy Mother of God, the apostles, Saint Martha, Saint Mary Magdalene, Marcella,[38] and many other disciples of Jesus, both male and female. Suddenly, a thunderous sound resonated throughout the entire chamber. A multitude of brilliant lights appeared, resembling tongues of fire. These fiery tongues settled over the heads of each one of them.

All of them were filled with the Holy Spirit and began to speak in numerous different languages and dialects. The commotion of all of this could be observed clearly from beyond the house, and at once a multitude gathered to observe what was happening. The apostles then went forth and addressed this crowd, preaching the word of God to them. They did this in numerous different languages, according to the gift of the Holy

---

[38] This Marcella was, according to tradition, the maidservant in the household of Martha, Mary Magdalene, and Lazarus. See chapters 12 and 13.

Spirit, and with such fervor and freedom that they seemed to many observers to be intoxicated.

All the crowds marveled at this. But there were a few who mocked them, saying: "These men are clearly drunk!" And then she saw the apostles go forth throughout the city of Jerusalem, proclaiming the Resurrection of the Christ, and that He was the true Son of God.

When this vision concluded and Veronica returned to her senses, she found that all the sisters were seated together for the festive luncheon to mark the Solemnity of Pentecost. As for Veronica herself, she felt that her whole mind, body, and soul were filled with the Holy Spirit, and her heart melted within her with spiritual joy.

As Blessed Veronica entered the chapel to prayer after the festive meal, one of the other nuns, named Sister Thadea,[39] embraced her, for she sensed that she was filled with the fire of divine love. She felt the body of Veronica to be filled with a miraculous and indescribable warmth of celestial sweetness, which passed into her own body and soul. And she knew that Blessed Veronica had received that day a rare and precious gift from her beloved Spouse, Jesus Christ, the King of Heaven and Earth; to whom be glory forever and ever! Amen.

---

[39] It was this Sister Thadea with whom Blessed Veronica shared her visions. Sister Thadae then related them to Fr. Isidor Isolanus, OP, who compiled them in writing.

Representation of St. Veronica of Milan

19th century engraving of the Blessed Mother appearing to St. Veronica of Milan